PLAY YOURSELF
BY HARRY KONDOLEON

★

DRAMATISTS
PLAY SERVICE
INC.

PLAY YOURSELF was produced by the New York Theatre Workshop (James C. Nicola, Artistic Director; Lynn Moffat, Managing Director; Linda S. Chapman, Associate Artistic Director). It opened at the Century Center for the Performing Arts in New York City on July 10, 2002. It was directed by Craig Lucas; the set design was by John McDermott; the lighting design was by Ben Stanton; the original music and sound design were by David Van Tieghem; the costume design was by Catherine Zuber; and the production stage manager was Antonia Gianino. The cast was as follows:

SELMA .... Ann Guilbert
HARMON .... Juan Carlos Hernandez
MARYVONNE .... Elizabeth Marvel
JEAN .... Marian Seldes

CHARACTERS

SELMA

HARMON

MARYVONNE

JEAN

TIME

1986.

PLAY YOURSELF

ACT ONE

Scene 1

Morning.

YVONNE. Are you ready for breakfast? Breakfast breakfast breakfast. Sweetheart, make an appearance. *(Enter Jean.)*
JEAN. Darling, when you shout at me like that I know I'm alive, please don't do it.
YVONNE. Oats, wheat, cream of rice, which is it today?
JEAN. I couldn't sleep again. A lot of bad dialogue going through my head as usual.
YVONNE. *Mean To Me?*
JEAN. Yeah.
YVONNE. The first scene where he loves her?
JEAN. No, the last scene where he dumps her. You know, *Get out! Get out, you can't stay here anymore, my wife's coming back?*
YVONNE. *Your wife? You're not married.*
JEAN. *Aren't I? Guess again.*
YVONNE. Wheat toast or pumpernickel?
JEAN. Yvonne, why don't you let me make it, just for a change. You know, I'm not completely useless. I practice when you go out.
YVONNE. Last year you set your robe on fire.
JEAN. So this one is fireproof. Let me serve you.
YVONNE. Sit down. Here's your tea. Sit down.
JEAN. She's wearing a black cocktail dress, bare legs. She's holding a bowl or a cup or something and it slips from her hand but it doesn't break, it just sort of bounces. And then she crinkles up in her chair; she sees it in his face: he isn't joking and suddenly everything is gone:

5

youth, beauty, spring, everything that she thought was there.

YVONNE. Jam or not?

JEAN. That's not that sugarless kind is it —

YVONNE. No, that's mine. You're reaching for the wrong one. Not that one, this one. See, it's the one I put in your yogurt yesterday.

JEAN. Oh, that was delicious! Get me that, Yvonne. Forget the oats, just mix me up some of that jam with some nice cool yogurt. Never mind why she's wearing a black cocktail dress in the middle of the day. No one asked those kinds of questions.

YVONNE. Maybe the man comes back to her or another *nicer* one shows up that makes her glad the first one went away.

JEAN. Are you kidding? She's smashed up for good that one. Although it's not in the plot, I know the rest of it! The weeping, the replaying old conversations until they're not conversations at all anymore but demented prayers; if that's love, I'm glad I never fell in it. Yvonne, get the mail.

YVONNE. I already did. It's on the table. There's something from Bobby in there.

JEAN. Something from Bobby, oh good! Come on already, Jesus! How long does it take to mix a glass of some jelly and some yogurt — you'd think I asked you for something hard to do.

YVONNE. I'm taking an extra long time because you're bullying me. Here.

JEAN. Read me what Bobby says. Where is he?

YVONNE. I don't know why you're in such a rush to hear what Bobby's got to say. From his various hot spots all we get are complaints of a world that looked better in photographs. Bobby's advice to the world: stay home.

JEAN. You didn't go out last night. Why?

YVONNE. Can I get you some more red goop or have you had enough?

JEAN. Most nights you go out late, stay out later, come back sometimes not until morning and I'm glad because I assume you're having a good time and are happy and I only want you to be happy, Yvonne, that's my only wish. I don't know where you go, who you meet there, what you do when you get together and I'm not asking — you're way beyond the age that you have to report to me, as if I was ever that type.

YVONNE. Most mothers want their daughter to stay home.

JEAN. Name one. I want you to go out. You spend entirely too much time babysitting for me, Yvonne. Come nightfall, I'm under the covers. I've got the radio, candy in the drawer, Kleenex, sleep or no sleep I'm all set.

YVONNE. How did we get on this subject?

JEAN. I don't expect you to meet anyone nice. All the nice people have died. They died before even I was born. I only hope they're all happy with one another in their other world.

YVONNE. Ha ha, it's not a letter, just a postcard in an envelope. "Dear Jean and Yvonne." You see how he always puts your name first — he's really your friend, I'm just an appendage.

JEAN. Just read. Is this my tea?

YVONNE. Yeah, sorry, I just drank it by accident. "Dear Jean and Yvonne, today we got out at Monte Carlo. It is not the Monte Carlo of lore and although I dare not say so to Gregory who thinks these are the Arabian Nights, Monte Carlo and all other cities and seaports we have visited seem to me as tacky and boring as the shopping malls of the Midwest I fled. Of course I don't let on to my excited partner what a snooze the trip is and risk blowing my status as agreeable. God knows in the marriage industry, and I use the term loosely, one must make do with what one has and I know, Yvonne, you disapprove of me for that and all I can say is that you really shouldn't and that I like Gregory in my own way. So there. Enclosed please find, Jean, a weird newspaper clipping about you. A family of little scholars passed through the hotel lobby yesterday and left in their dreary wake a pile of Sunday Book Review sections and I found this. You see, there really is no place to hide. Kisses and love from Bobby. Gregory says hello."

JEAN. All that fit on a postcard?

YVONNE. He wrote on both sides. Get a load of this newspaper clipping.

JEAN. Let me guess. There's yet another cult celebrating my brief appearances in a stack of mysteriously self-erasing films. Give them my best regards and tell them to reconsider some other poor soul or better yet just have them honor what's-her-name again. Now she's gone she can endure the torture of being shaken from oblivion's lilypad.

YVONNE. A woman named Selma something-or-other wants anyone who knows anything about the star of *Beat the Band, Love Match* and *Mean To Me* to kindly communicate with her. There's an address. She must think you're dead.

JEAN. I wasn't in *Beat the Band*.

YVONNE. Of course you were. If you're through with these dishes

I'll take them in. They changed the title six times but then settled on *Beat the Band*. I'm doing laundry today, tell me what you wanted cleaned.

JEAN. There's a small pile at the foot of my bed.

YVONNE. I got that.

JEAN. Maybe we should write this character Selma.

YVONNE. What for?

JEAN. If she does think I'm dead, we can have a bit of fun with her.

YVONNE. Fun? You *are* bored.

JEAN. Get a piece of paper and we'll compose a letter.

YVONNE. Sit down, you're going to knock something over.

JEAN. Did you move that table?

YVONNE. Sweetie pie, I didn't move a thing, now sit down.

JEAN. Now I remember. Clunky music, goopy lyrics, bad costumes, bad dialogue, bad everything. Originally it was going to be called *Good At It* which I guess was supposed to have some dirty connotation but they took one look at it and no one was good at anything so they changed the title to *Beat the Band*. I sang "Bye Bye Blackbird" — badly — and never mind that there were about twelve other pictures that year with people singing the same song.

YVONNE. Sit down.

JEAN. What are you doing? Maryvonne, answer me.

YVONNE. I'm writing your letter.

JEAN. Read me what you have.

YVONNE. "Dear Selma, what a joy it was catching your ad in one of the Sunday sections. My daughter and I pore —"

JEAN. My daughter and I! I like that, ghost writer!

YVONNE. "My daughter and I pore over all sections pertaining to entertainment as we are both big entertainment buffs. The truth is we know intimately the woman you inquire after and hope only that our insights might entertain you enough to make your visit worthwhile, say for tea, Tuesday the fourth. Train schedule enclosed."

JEAN. And sign it.

YVONNE. We can use your real name since she obviously doesn't know it or she would have used it.

JEAN. That's true.

YVONNE. "Good luck, Maryvonne and Jean."

JEAN. Don't put in good luck! You want to scare her away before she gets here?

YVONNE. Best wishes or sincerely?

JEAN. Sincerely.

YVONNE. Sealed.

JEAN. I hope she comes. I hope she comes and she has a beautiful brother for you, Yvonne —

YVONNE. What — are you nuts?!

JEAN. Yes I do, Yvonne, because you're getting cold, very cold, and I'm afraid for you.

YVONNE. Close-up. I stand as if lifted by invisible ropes. I've just read the letter my lover has sent me. It says it's all over, I drop the letter. I laugh to myself a gallows laugh, he'll come back on his knees and then it'll be my turn to be mean.

JEAN. You're getting too much like me and that's a crime for a girl as young and beautiful as yourself.

YVONNE. I'm neither.

JEAN. What are you saying — are you crazy? Every time I'm forced to talk to someone in this godforgotten neighborhood they mumble to me how beautiful you are!

YVONNE. You've got the scenario all wrong.

JEAN. Listen to me! I don't want you to be my housekeeper, Yvonne. I have two cents in the bank, I can have someone come in for a penny and change the pillowcases. I don't want you to do anything else for me. Yvonne, it's killing me, do you hear me, you're going to stand over my grave and say I killed my mother if you don't stop minding me, Yvonne, and go out and do whatever people do to enjoy life.

YVONNE. One more word and I don't mail the letter.

JEAN. Yes, I hope she comes with a beautiful brother and you marry him and that she's such a hopeless drudge she stays here and vacuums for me. That's what I hope.

Scene 2

Tuesday the fourth.

SELMA. I can't talk I'm so impressed with all the information you have. It's uncanny, whenever I'm on the receiving end of so many confidences I can never concentrate. I don't know why but today I'm absorbing it all up. You know, I thought I was the world's biggest expert on this particular person and could, as they say, write the book, but, my goodness, what you don't know. You seem to know it all and then some. Dialogue at your fingertips. Am I glad I came and, you know something, I almost didn't. I showed your note to someone who said it was sarcastic.

YVONNE. More tea, Selma?

SELMA. No thanks. I trembled on the train coming up. I trembled and trembled because I was having a date with destiny.

YVONNE. It's four-thirty, the last train's at five, don't you have to go now?

SELMA. Oh, I hope not.

YVONNE. Well, we were glad to have you, Selma, and wish you all the luck in the world. Let's see, were you wearing a coat? Here it is.

JEAN. Selma, how is it you say you're an expert on this particular person and you haven't figured out all afternoon you've been looking right at her?

SELMA. You?

JEAN. That's right, I'm me. The studio made up that other name. Anyone who knows me calls me Jean.

SELMA. You're you?

JEAN. And this is my daughter Maryvonne.

YVONNE. Hello. Didn't we do this scene already?

SELMA. I thought you were dead.

JEAN. Did you ever read an obituary?

SELMA. No.

JEAN. Well then I'm not dead. I can't look that different. There must be some shred of my face left intact, some intonation in the voice. Even I would have recognized me and I'm half-blind.

SELMA. As Brother Harmon says, and I repeat after him, you turn a corner and you turn yet another corner and there it is, the very thing you've been looking for, waiting for you!

YVONNE. Brother who?

JEAN. Whose brother?

SELMA. Oh Jean, then it's all worked out for the best!

JEAN. What has?

SELMA. Why I'm here.

JEAN. Why?

SELMA. Why did you think I was here?

JEAN. I don't know. I thought you were writing a book.

SELMA. Oh no, I would never write a book! I know I must seem like one of those people who know everything about Hollywood because their own lives have no excitement but I must tell you I have a life of exceeding fascination! In fact, where I go I never mention the movies because they're just too tiny in the face of what I do.

YVONNE. What do you do?

SELMA. I work with the hopeless! Yes, the hopeless. Such an undertaking requires, yes, stamina, but more important than that, courage, courage way beyond my faint capacity and so to advance even baby steps in this colossal undertaking, we — for I don't work alone — are led by a beautiful man of great moral strength.

YVONNE. And you two work together in the streets helping bums?

SELMA. Oh, we work in a building, Yvonne, in the center of town and there are many of us helpers, and the people who come there, Yvonne, are not just bums, I can assure you.

YVONNE. And this guy, your leader, he's cute? Does he make house calls? I know quite a few hopeless characters who have trouble getting into town.

JEAN. Oh, be quiet, Yvonne, this is interesting. Tell us, Selma dear, about this man. You say he's very good looking and charismatic, is that Brother Harmon.

SELMA. Oh yes. I'll have another cup of tea.

YVONNE. But it's room temperature now, you don't want it. Oh look, the pot's empty.

SELMA. Jean, I've been spending all my savings putting ads in papers and visiting total strangers collecting information on you. I have a whole folder but I don't need it anymore, I can throw it away. The fact is I can watch you and listen to you and then be you.

YVONNE. Ma!

SELMA. Up to now I've never appeared as anything but myself, but I've always dreamt I could be someone else, and now it's going to come true!

YVONNE. Ma —

SELMA. I saw you a few years ago at two o'clock in the morning — on TV — in a movie and then again the next night in another one — and though you're always left behind you're always there again — and I said to myself, that one, she's very deep, if I could be her and stand up in front of aloof people and tell them, you know, "Look at me, dumped over and over, and I keep on coming back for more, in picture after picture," that life's worth living and all, that it would really work, that it would give people more hope.

YVONNE. Ma —

JEAN. And he'd come here if you asked him to, this fellow — isn't he too busy, what with all the hopeless customers in the world?

SELMA. He'd come if I told him it was you here. He's a bigger fan than I am. He knows dialogue by heart, too.

WOMAN. Two on a match is bad luck, isn't it?

MAN. Not if it's a *love match*.

WOMAN. I imagine you say that to all the girls.

MAN. No, only the ones I love.

WOMAN. The ones?

MAN. The one. I do love you.

WOMAN. Just like that?

MAN. You're my type.

WOMAN. What type is that?

MAN. You. Look in the mirror. No, make my eyes your mirror. Look — come closer. Closer sti —

JEAN. They kiss.

YVONNE. Ma —

JEAN. Sweetheart, go into the kitchen and get something out for supper, Selma's joining us. Cocktail, Selma? You know, I never drank because my grandmother was a big drunk and I didn't want to be like her. When I told her I was going to be an actress she said, "Fools' names and fools' faces always appear in public places!" Not drinking made me very unpopular at Hollywood parties; everyone would be laughing away and I'd think, what's the big joke?

YVONNE. You're going to spill that.

JEAN. Darling, you're wanted in the kitchen. Go there now. *(Yvonne goes into the kitchen.)* Okay, now, first of all, Selma, I cannot call you that name, it's just too awful and I'm going to change it for you and in time if not right away you'll thank me. Let's see, how about Betty? Betty's not bad. Your name is Betty. With a Y. So this guy, Betty, he's not your brother is he?

SELMA. Oh, no.

JEAN. He's just someone who helps these people at this hostel you work at, what is it, a kind of soup kitchen?

SELMA. It supplies free food and some lodging, clothes, and arranges health care for the sick, poor and homeless.

JEAN. But, Betty, there's something more extraordinary about this place, isn't there? You say it gives people hope who have none left?

SELMA. And more than that! Faith. It's given it to me.

JEAN. And you say this guy is responsible.

SELMA. Well, I am too, all of us who work at the house, we help people, give them hope.

JEAN. But now, Betty, come closer, you have to be reasonable. You expect me to tell you all I know, every last detail, you know: which top female stars made passes at me, which marriages were the biggest farces of them all and who had the biggest pecker in Hollywood. You expect me to tell you all that and more and then have you mimic me, ape my gestures and, what? go into some arena and sell tickets or whatever you have in mind — and with no recompense for me? If you were me, Betty, you would have to ask yourself, as I ask myself, what's in it for me? *(Yvonne leaves the kitchen.)* What did you take out for dinner?

YVONNE. Chicken, fish, I don't know, I couldn't recognize it.

JEAN. Well, whatever it is, go back into the kitchen and do something to it.

YVONNE. There's nothing to do, we're having it plain.

SELMA. Don't fuss for me, why at home sometimes I only have a potato.

YVONNE. If my mother's promising to tell you scintillating stories of movieland, I warn you she can't remember any names or dates or even titles of things correctly.

JEAN. Yvonne's jealous because she was a type of performer too at one time and similarly retired. A stripper.

YVONNE. I was not a stripper!

JEAN. Call it what you like, I'm not saying I disapproved. I only say the gods arranged for me to have impaired vision before I could behold this spectacle.

YVONNE. Oh very funny. I was not a stripper. I danced on bar tops with my friend Bobby. We had the same costume, horsetails coming out of our backsides. He wore an old pair of underpants and I had a sort of broken-down corset. You know, it wasn't supposed to be taken seriously, it was sort of artistic, ironic, you know, like a goof or gag, only esoteric and we do it, at night, late, Thursdays and Sundays for fifty dollars and drinks, first at a club on White Street and then when that got tired some place on C that practically caved in around us. I mean we didn't sing or anything, just danced in place to records while everyone walked around drinking. Anyway this was a million years ago and we were both over-the-hill at the time. Forget it.

JEAN. If you can. Now, Betty, I want you to listen and forget whatever lightweight dribble I told you before when I still thought you were some little autograph hound here to poke a pen at an old stack of bones.

YVONNE. And what do you think now? *Betty?* Who's Betty?

13

JEAN. Clam up, Yvonne, I'm going into a monologue. Ready? People, and I don't care who, do not want to play themselves. Get me? The part's too close to them. And I don't care if you're talking about the movies or real life. And once you appear as something, *it sticks.* You develop a reputation and — the public won't accept you as anything else. You fit a category, get me? Flashback. It's the year zero, I'm right out of school and my mother takes me to see this talent scout. I was very pretty with hair down to here like an angel so my mother must have meant it like a compliment — Well, the next thing I know I'm told I'm playing the part of the girlfriend. Well, isn't that nice. I hadn't even had a boyfriend yet. The first thing they do is cut my hair off up to here. I'm in a black dress cut down to here, and the "boy" I'm supposed to make love to is three times my age wearing more pancake than I am and in the plot is a married man. The long and the short of it is the guy dumps me and goes back to his wife.

SELMA. *Mean To Me.*

JEAN. Yeah, *Mean To Me.* A big success. And from that day forward that is what I played, some variation on the woman the man strays to and eventually flees. A famous actress at the time, a Russian, she took me into her dressing room and she said, "My dear, how does it feel to have lived your whole life before the age of seventeen?" She knew, I'd been *typed.* I was a virgin. I don't mean I didn't know what was going on on earth; I was a voracious reader encouraged by both my parents and knew whatever there was to find out in books but I was innocent, see? Where did you go?

SELMA. I'm here.

JEAN. The directors were always howling off to the side, "Play yourself, just play yourself!" — and you know in those days anyone could be a director and I mean *anyone,* just some kid who happened to be strolling by the set. Play myself, I was a goody-goody from some out-of-the-way town — I knew *Mother Goose* by heart! — and I was cast repeatedly as these — I don't know what to call them, they weren't vamps — just women who got in the way of happy endings and had to be shot, locked up, sent off or just — as was the case most frequently — just dropped from the plot entirely with no real resolution, in a word, lost. Where are you?

SELMA. Here.

JEAN. I thought the movies I was in would somehow reflect where I was in my life or what I believed in but that was an *unrealistic expectation,* one of many. I called a book I wrote *Unrealistic*

Expectations: Goodbye! I burned it. The last chapter was the poop on everyone in the business. The only person who wouldn't have sued me would've been myself. You see, I came eventually to think of myself as the woman I was forced to portray and I became that in my own life: left out of the plot, marginal, extraneous, not happy.

YVONNE. Can I pour you another one, *Betty?*

JEAN. I begged them to let me play something else, just for once someone normal — you know that's the hardest thing. Anyone can put on a wig and sneer at people. I asked Evelyn Brent — and she was old at the time — I said, "Evelyn, didn't you get tired of playing the same thing over and over?" — gun molls. "No," she says. And then they killed her with that one movie and off to the Motion Picture Home she goes! So before I could be killed by the box office I quit, quit playing sadsacks and slatterns in plots of hopped-up hooey. I'll go to sunny hell before I go back to California! If I didn't have my daughter where would I be? Where are you?

YVONNE. Here.

SELMA. You have your hands on my face.

JEAN. You're not very pretty. Too bad. That's not easily forgiven. That and success. And failure. They're not easily forgiven. Bring me this handsome man, Harmon. I want to meet him. I want to meet one handsome man before I die, I'm tired, excuse me.

YVONNE. Take your nap now. Dinner in thirty minutes. *(Jean exits.)*

SELMA. What happened to her eyes?

YVONNE. Accident with eye drops. She said it was the makeup man ... she can see light and dark but blurry. Just the shape of things. Don't you think you should go home now?

SELMA. I'm going to help her. I'm going to give her faith. I learned to do that. Your mother asked me what was in it for her, what she would get in return. That's what I can do, I can help her.

YVONNE. Is that so? Usually I take a nap around now too but I'm not tired. I don't go out at night anymore. I used to go out every night and stay out very late.

SELMA. I can sleep here.

YVONNE. Yes, sometimes I'd sleep on that couch if the guy's apartment was too far away and I didn't want to go and I would never have him into my room. I wanted to always keep the sheets clean for me.

SELMA. Maybe I can go into the kitchen, help dinner along.

YVONNE. No, leave it alone, dinner helps itself. My mother wishes I was going out more often. I don't know where she thought I went or what she thought I did but unless you like hanging out at shopping malls, and I'm a little old for that, there really is no place to go except creepy, local, and curiously antiseptic bars. After a while I think I was recognized. "She'll go to bed with you once, maybe twice, but no more." College students, married men, wanderers, I had a big turnover. "I love you" was something I heard often. Have you ever heard that?

SELMA. No.

YVONNE. No, I didn't think so. Sit down I'll tell you about yourself. You're an extra. Nothing is happening for you and from all you can judge now nothing is ever likely to happen and that knowledge has brought you desperation and there's something admirable I think in desperation, anyway; right before it takes you over. But that's the trick, how far away from yourself you can go and still come back. Hmm, Betty? You play me.

SELMA. Play you? I don't know you.

YVONNE. Improvise. I walk into the bar.

SELMA. I come into the bar. It's crowded. People are laughing and shaking each other's hands. When everyone sees me, they put down their drinks and say, "Hi, Selma!" I mean, "Hi, Yvonne."

YVONNE. I walk into the bar. It's half empty as usual. I have a glass of club soda. I don't drink while I'm there. I've already smoked some pot in the parking lot across the street to relax. A school teacher comes up to me. He has the same miserable numbing problems of everyone who doesn't like his job, doesn't like his wife, doesn't like his girlfriend, doesn't like his shoes. And we walk out to his car.

SELMA. I'm kissed there, kissed and kissed and kissed.

YVONNE. Fade out. Flash forward. Six months later, I'm in the bar again.

SELMA. Everyone tells me they missed me.

YVONNE. I'm talking to a student. He wants to move to New York. He's fascinated by the club scene. I tell him how I used to dance on bar tops with a horsetail. The schoolteacher comes in. He wants to talk to me.

SELMA. "I love you," he says.

YVONNE. No, you play me. You sit still. Close-up on the man. "Why haven't you called me," he says. "I think you gave me the wrong number by accident — what's wrong with you, I thought

16

we hit it off. Were you just faking?" You say you're embarrassing me in front of my friend.

SELMA. Is it the teacher of the student?

YVONNE. What? I don't know. That's not the point. You're a bad student, Selma. How are you going to know what it's like to be someone else if you keep interjecting your little aspirations into the story? Now, locate whatever performer instincts you have and hold onto them; in a good performance as in a good audience there's always something held back, something not given, if you surrender completely you're thought of as a type of fool. All right, I'll be me and you play the man.

SELMA. What man?

YVONNE. Any man! That's the point. Any man at all.

SELMA. And what do I say?

YVONNE. That you love me.

SELMA. Why?

YVONNE. Because you're a man! You're driven to say things like that. You just say it.

SELMA. I love you.

YVONNE. Well, I don't love you.

SELMA. You tricked me!

YVONNE. That's the point. You get the fly into the net and then you don't eat it. There's no point to it, you just sit back and do it, it's called remote control.

SELMA. It's a great loss, I'm sure, to lose from weakness or circumstance a person you love, a pain from a lost love remains worse than anything. Don't you think so, Yvonne?

YVONNE. Where did that come from? About lost love I wouldn't know, I've already told you I've never been in love.

SELMA. That's can't be true.

YVONNE. It is true, believe me, I've experimented enough to know. And now I'll never know otherwise because I've been on a *resolve*. I don't go out anymore. Ten days ago my low opinion of myself and of life had come to a sort of climax or nadir depending on your point of view and I wanted to freeze it there where it was comfortable — to feel no worse so I wouldn't kill myself and feel no better so I wouldn't seek to improve matters. And I think it's all very well-timed before I lose my looks. Isn't there some philosopher or greengrocer who said the secret to tasting good forever is to stop being eaten when you taste the best? Perhaps that's the secret to sex. Anyway there's some safety in stopping before you're the one rejected. That would be too nasty a turn in the plot — the joke would be on me that time.

SELMA. I won't go, Yvonne, I'm a very strong person.

YVONNE. How about a visual aid? It's a Polaroid from a gentleman who happened to have all kinds of equipment lying about. Look at it. The angle's like that because I was holding the camera while at the same time participating. Either way an unusual position, don't you think so? See the look in my eyes? I give everyone that dead stare, it frightens them but it's really because I never wear my contacts.

SELMA. You're only frightening yourself, Maryvonne.

YVONNE. *(Empties out Selma's handbag.)* What's in here? What does a character like you carry around with her anyway-cookies-for-later and a lot of wrinkled-up shit.

SELMA. Leave my bag alone! You're a very unpleasant girl!

YVONNE. Yeah, I know! I keep breaking the unwritten law of America — *"Thou Shalt Not Be Unpleasant."* They should put it on the steps of the Capitol. What are all these combs? And all these lipsticks. Tell me, Miss Fuller Hope Lady, out of curiosity, what exactly is your strategy? ... Do you and Brother Harmon paint happy faces on people and comb their hair? Look, here's some money, take it to cover your car fare. My mother and I played a joke on you and it's backfired: suddenly nothing's funny.

SELMA. You're not who you say you are?

YVONNE. Oh, we are, that's the grisly punch line. If it's too much take a cab from the terminal and think of us. I know you just want to sympathize and I guess that's a good hobby — I envy you because I have no sympathy for anyone, least of all myself. I guess instead of a heart I've got a tick, a chigger, the kind of bug you pick off coats with tweezers.

SELMA. I'm a shoplifter. I shoplift. It's the only thing I can really do well: steal things. I can move my hand over something and it disappears, it goes in my bag or pockets. See? This is me. *(Demonstrates her skill at stealing.)* I started stealing a long time ago. I started going into stores and taking things. I don't know what, *junk,* little scented candles, costume jewelry I would be ashamed to wear, combs, lipstick. I had phony credit cards and then had garage sales from the things I stole. I did it every Saturday until the police came. How does an unmarried woman have a garage sale every week, said the judge. *(Jean switches on a light which illuminates her; she has been listening.)*

JEAN. Maryvonne, forget dinner, I'm not hungry. My daughter

and I have lost our taste for living. Can you save me?

SELMA. I'm a fake! I'm a fake. I have no faith, no faith at all. I just pretend to have faith, and hope it will come one day, I have none!

YVONNE. A letter came before from Bobby and I was saving it. Shall I open it now and read it to you?

JEAN. A letter will take too long, Yvonne, we haven't got time. Call him now, Betty, this Brother Harmon, let's have him here now.

End of Act One

ACT TWO

Scene 1

Some time has passed — days.

JEAN. How nice to hear someone's life story in one gulp and be included so considerately in it. Thank you.

HARMON. It's an honor to meet you. Not many things would get me away from my work.

JEAN. Yes, well, now I'd like to know more about your little establishment for making people feel better about themselves.

HARMON. There, you've said it all, that's all we ever actually do, make people feel better about themselves, nothing else. I'm not saying it's easy, of course. A lot of people get pretty banged up in life and it takes more patience and love to set them right than many are willing to offer but that's only because they too are banged up from life, but by getting one to help another everyone eventually gets built up again.

JEAN. And you're the one who sets this whole cycle of love in motion? I must say it sounds sexy. But basically, and I beg you in advance not to think me rude for saying so, basically all you do is lie to everyone: tell them it's all going to work out when in fact you know it's all a big mess, that everyone's sliding downhill fast and that unless you're a car thief or a pickpocket you can bet by sundown you'll be traveling by foot empty-handed.

HARMON. You don't believe that.

JEAN. Maybe I do and maybe I don't. Either way you have to take into account I'm not in the rush of things anymore and haven't been for some time so perhaps things have changed. That's possible, radical change in the world. Don't you agree Yvonne? Yvonne, you're still in the room, aren't you?

YVONNE. I'm here. I'm not very fond of talk. I prefer less civilized pastimes. I'll list them if you're interested.

JEAN. We can all guess, Yvonne. Pass these *(The cookies.)* around.

Betty's been taking very good care of us, we're quite spoiled.

HARMON. Has she been cooking?

JEAN. Oh sure … What are these cookies you keep making I never heard of before?

SELMA. Tollhouse.

JEAN. See, I really am in a time warp. More tea, please. Now, don't get Yvonne wrong, man-with-the-nice-voice, but you have to understand her background, growing up with me. Am I filled? Great. I mean working for two decades in Never-Never Land, one brief crummy marriage — Yvonne's not from that marriage, no, that wouldn't have been possible in that combo. And, you know, in Hollywood, they didn't like women having babies, you're supposed to adopt them to keep your image or your figure, I forget which. Nothing was supposed to have passed through your legs but tulle and fairy dust. I had a helluva time having Yvonne — here I was, not young, not married anymore, the father a bit-part player who first says *I love you* — famous last words — and then tells me about his wife and kids — trick characters that pop up in the plot when you need them. Well, you know. So I'm sent to this doctor the studio has for people who mismanage their contraception but at the last minute I get it into my head that it would be "bad for my soul" — that's original, isn't it? During the pregnancy I had to go right on shooting — that's how I perfected that famous suffering look — I was squeezed into a girdle to flatten poor little Yvonne — I passed out three times and when I was too far along they had me stand behind desks and barrels. They should have just let me walk across the screen big as a house as a precautionary message. So here I am playing tarts, and sure enough everyone starts believing me to be this character so I'm asked out *all the time* and because I always said no and wouldn't sleep with anyone, the press agents started this rumor that I was a lesbian. Now, mind you, Hollywood hated lesbians although lesbian circles thrived everywhere you turned — I mean your wig would fall off if I gave you a list of the names. But as far as power's concerned it was a town absolutely run by men with the exception of those — two satanic hags — Hedda and what's the other one, Loulabell — but there's a special hell waiting for people who get a kick out of other people's misfortunes — and then of course most of the time they would just make things up, just *lie.* The men wanted the women to be "good listeners" which in the case of many meant crouching under the desks of studio heads during conferences and, make note, they did not stick you under there to look for paper clips. Fade-out. So much for tea. Time to switch to wine. Where's my bottle? Would you care for some wine, Brother Harmon? White wine? Betty, you get it.

HARMON. Thank you.

JEAN. I'm a white wino. Now I'll stop and someone else speak. One grows so tired of one's neverending saga, don't you think so, Brother Harmon? Yvonne, you say something.

YVONNE. I said I have nothing to say.

JEAN. Read Bobby's letter. Yvonne and I have a friend named Bobby who's very controversial in this house, we love him. He's gone off with a tax lawyer and I say more power to him but Yvonne says since Bobby's not in love and is therefore engaging on some level in a kind of deception —

YVONNE. With himself.

JEAN. Right, that it's an all around bad deal. Now, what's your opinion? Read the letter, Yvonne.

YVONNE. "Dear Jean and Yvonne, we are now in Biarritz — "

JEAN. They're on a vacation.

YVONNE. " — in a huge hotel that costs a fortune. It looks at the Atlantic Ocean, only from the other side. The sun is bright and glaring but there's much talk of a great show of fireworks tonight so maybe I should have waited until then to begin this letter and cast it in better light. A beautiful woman in the lobby said that Biarritz is the Borscht Belt of France. Where did she pick up that expression? The rate of spending we do daily scares me. I have too many new shirts and I scheme at night about sewing them into a big tent and living in the desert and chanting shanti. There's something weirdly hysterical about someone as conservative as Gregory going spend-crazy. Next door someone's singing all the songs from the Beatles' *White Album* one after the other in order. I hope it stops soon as it is very downbeat without the music. Lots of love from Bobby. Gregory says hello."

HARMON. I think you're too critical of yourself.

JEAN. Critical of myself? I'm not critical of myself, I'm critical of everyone else.

HARMON. You're not really surprised when people behave abominably, are you?

JEAN. Should I be?

HARMON. Absolutely not.

JEAN. I should expect it.

HARMON. Anything you can expect you can get.

YVONNE. You mean like Lotto?

JEAN. Hey, you didn't say anything about Bobby's letter!

HARMON. What's there to say?

SELMA. It gets my goat that I've spent most of my life barely able to scrape up busfare to get to the corner and then this Bobby person complains when he gets a free trip to Europe.

YVONNE. Oh Betty, you missed the whole point.

HARMON. Why do you call Selma Betty?

SELMA. I don't mind.

JEAN. She likes it.

HARMON. Now, Jean, and may I call you Jean? You worked in an extremely high-powered industry and like any industry it's a money-making operation, so don't you think it was innocent of you not to perceive the limitations of your function? If you played a tart and the tart you played helped the picture you were in make money, it only makes sense you'd be hired again and again until that tart ceased to be attached to a money-making mechanism, if you follow me.

JEAN. You're suggesting — and it's because you're young and must only have a passing familiarity with the world — that one operates within a system of choices. Well, my dear Brother Harmon, there is very often only one way to turn. I had a baby girl, no father for it and no husband.

HARMON. You had a baby with a man you have almost nothing to say about. Why?

JEAN. One craves physical affection at least momentarily if not periodically; with many it's constantly. Am I to be pilloried for that? Betty, get my cough drops from my night table, my throat's dry. (Selma exits.)

HARMON. You mustn't talk to her as if she were the servant, whether she's here to help you or help herself or whether she seems weak and eager for punishment. She's a lovely person and I respect and like her. (Selma enters with cough drops.)

SELMA. Here, Jean.

JEAN. Thank you.

HARMON. And of course I'm not prudish or conventional enough to be recommending only the lawfully wedded bear children. I only say, for myself, I would no sooner get into bed with someone I didn't love as, I don't know what, as jump in a pot of boiling water. I'm not pretending to be so ignorant of human circumstance as to not know why the million things that happen to people happen. It's because we become bored and hysterical because we don't know what we're doing or why we're doing it.

JEAN. Does anyone know what he's talking about?

YVONNE. He's saying the reality you endorse is that reality that comes back to you. Like a bad check. Is that what you're saying, Brother Harmon?

HARMON. You needn't call me Brother Harmon if it's so absurd to you. It's just a name that caught on where I work. My last name is Harmon but you can call me Larry.

JEAN. I don't know about this the-reality-you-believe-in-is-the-one-that-is jazz; all I know is people believe what they see.

HARMON. Then show them something else.

JEAN. But that's what I keep trying to tell everyone — you get stuck! That's why I quit.

HARMON. Weren't you fired?

JEAN. Fired or quit. When it's time for you to go, my dear, your bags pack themselves.

YVONNE. Sandwich anyone?

JEAN. Are they those little things Bobby used to make with the crusts cut off? Give me one.

YVONNE. Here.

JEAN. Now, I'm sure it would be very dandy for us to sit here all afternoon and exchange gossip from our respective realities but the reason you were invited here this afternoon was to advise us on the subject which is supposedly your particular occupation and calling, and that is faith. And I say faith in that chatty birdlike manner because I suffer from drastic lapses of it.

HARMON. Faith in what?

JEAN. In everything, in merely going on, in fundamentally all activities great and small. What practical advice do you have for me, Harmon?

HARMON. Come to our hostel and clean the floors, peel carrots, stir the soup, teach people to sing songs, let someone who has no one to talk to tell you their story.

JEAN. I'm leaving this address next in a casket — I haven't got time to peel carrots! I want to know what's going to make me feel better now.

HARMON. When people come to me in a state of emergency I have them sit down and write on a piece of paper The Right and Proper Thing To Do. On it the person lists what's right and wrong with their life and what they'd like to achieve and overcome. *My dear, I've come for you.*

JEAN. *It isn't too late, too late to say you love me, that you'll take me away —*

SELMA. It's *Mean To Me,* second scene from the end!

JEAN. Yvonne, change the lights, change the lighting.

SELMA. *I'm Mary, his wife. Please let him go, don't make him suffer.*

JEAN. *Oh, this is very humiliating, her here now too?*

HARMON. *I came for you but not to take you away. I'm going back to her. We can't see each other anymore. It's finished.*

JEAN. *Yes, finished.* Yvonne — feed me lines, feed me the lines.

YVONNE.	SELMA.
I thought you loved me.	I thought you loved me.
	I thought you loved me.

JEAN. *I thought you loved me, I thought you loved me. It's finished.*

SELMA. *Let her go.*

JEAN. *Then go.*

HARMON. *Goodbye.*

JEAN. I told them that scene needed to be expanded, that it was too choppy, that she had more fight in her and wouldn't collapse like that giving up!

HARMON. What soft and lovely hands you have and so fragrant.

JEAN. Fragrant I don't know but they're clean. Now if you'll excuse me I'll accept an escort from Betty or Selma, or whoever ... *(Selma and Jean exit.)*

HARMON. Your mother rants and raves but she doesn't mean what she says.

YVONNE. No?

HARMON. No, she's just pretending. She just wants you to leave without feeling guilty, it's obvious.

YVONNE. Leave? Leave where? I'm not going anywhere.

HARMON. Yes you are, you're coming with me. I'm in love with you.

YVONNE. Come again?

HARMON. I said I'm in love with you and we are going to go away together.

YVONNE. I'm sorry, I missed all the early Disney films so I don't know what you're quoting from.

HARMON. I'm not quoting from anything, I'm making it up as I go along, though I've rehearsed this scene in my head many times. I don't have to find out I love you; I merely had to recognize the person I have always loved but hadn't found yet, as you would with something you've misplaced before you were born.

YVONNE. Are you high?

HARMON. No, just happy, very happy.

YVONNE. And you love me?

HARMON. That's right.

YVONNE. Just like that.

HARMON. Yes.

YVONNE. I'm sorry, I'm not laughing at you, it's just that you can't appreciate the comedy in this.

HARMON. But I do.

YVONNE. You can't, you don't know me. I mean you're not the first person who's said I love you like that to me just flat out. I'm a magnet for love.

HARMON. You're lucky.

YVONNE. Let me finish. They love me but I don't love them.

HARMON. So much the better: you've been waiting for me.

YVONNE. No, no. I've had a hundred boyfriends, a hundred and one boyfriends. You see, I'm like one of the characters who come to your doorstep.

HARMON. You seem a little dismissive of them.

YVONNE. No more than of myself. It's just a pity you didn't show up sooner because usually that straightforward style works with me and I would've rewarded it by taking my clothes off and we could've made love right here. Just like that, I'm old-fashioned that way. It's a shame too because I find you attractive. But I'm on my new regime; no sex without love. But I've sunk myself into a sort of quagmire as I am suspicious of intimacy and the only thing I've found amusing up to now is athletic sex.

HARMON. You said up to now. What now do you find amusing?

YVONNE. What? I didn't say that.

HARMON. Yes you did.

YVONNE. No I didn't. I don't need you to tell me what's going on. I've solved my own problems and without the help of a shrink thank you just the same. My best friend Bobby — the one in Biarritz — and I used to dance in clubs with coffee cans tied to our ankles for tips and we kept a little scorecard of all our conquests — very Fifties — mine with the cute straight guys, Bobby with the cute gay guys. Bobby quit first because of ... the gay death that'll probably end up killing everyone and then it won't seem quite so gay. Anyway he's in Europe with his stuffy lawyer and I finally fig-ured out that unless you're a teenager, pointless sex-capades are just depressing. So I'm not going to bed with you.

HARMON. I already said I would no sooner sleep with someone who didn't love me than jump in a pot of boiling water.

YVONNE. Have you got one bubbling on the stove at all times to stave off temptation? Anyway what you said is that you wouldn't unless *you* were in love.

HARMON. But I want you to love me.

YVONNE. Ah yes, that's always the trick to the puzzle, getting the two pieces to fit at the same time.

HARMON. Strange that there are no photos on the walls or old posters or clippings.

YVONNE. They're in my room. I once went to bed with two guys who were best friends. I picked them up in a bar.

HARMON. So?

YVONNE. It was the best time I ever had. One was very shy so the other kept making encouraging remarks and I could concentrate on the one talking while the other one was busy and forget myself.

HARMON. Why would you want to do that?

YVONNE. Oh why why why, is that your way of helping people? You're sort of weird for a do-gooder. And I don't like the way you talked to my mother! I don't know who you think you are.

HARMON. And I don't know who you think I am, telling me old sex stories as if they're going to frighten me off. You must be very puritanical. Think how used to that sort of thing I must be anyway — people out of fear of getting any help always attempt to frighten you off. What were you going to tell me next, that you stood up on a high place with your skirt over your head?

YVONNE. I resent your presence here, it's sexist and degrading — three women and a guy who thinks he's Prince Charming.

HARMON. I don't like to argue. If you've been merely convinced, you'll become quickly unconvinced at the first doubt. I'm just going to sit patiently till you're ready.

YVONNE. You're nuts.

HARMON. Feel my fists. Aren't they strong? I used to beat up everything. I had a lot of anger because I had no natural talent for anything, not sports, scholastics, art. And since I was busy punching everyone, I wasn't particularly popular. The movies I swallowed I took as moral lessons and when their artificial system of justice didn't pan out in relation to life it was as if I'd cheated on a test and gotten all the wrong answers. I had no time for niceties. But rather than give up I worked twice as hard at everything. I had a Noah's

27

Ark idea that if I didn't excel I'd be left in the harbor.

YVONNE. Then what happened, you saw the face of Jesus on rodents and were converted?

HARMON. No, I excelled at everything but I still felt bad. And then I found out what my talent was. I had a great power — I could give people hope.

YVONNE. By lying to them?

HARMON. Don't have to, the truth is magic, you just say it and people stop believing in that other voice, the scratchy belittling one that says, "you'll never get anyone, you'll never get anyone, you'll never get — "

YVONNE. Oh, shut up. You're giving me a headache. Look, I'm sure what you do is very noble, shaking hands with untouchables or whatever you do, but — and I don't know what Selma's told you about me but I really don't need any help. Do you understand?

HARMON. Just like everybody else you want to be special for one person and have that person special for you. It was so easy for me to recognize you instantly. I've waited so long. It's as if I held your photo in my hand and matched your face to it. You're you: the one I love.

YVONNE. It's my mother's movies, her face in mine, that's all. Go find someone with a more interesting soul to play with. If you look into mine you won't see anything; it's an aquarium that's never been cleaned, no suckerfish and no snails — don't come near me!

HARMON. I didn't move.

YVONNE. Okay, here's the excuse I make for myself. Exposition exposition exposition. When I was little, although I was far more pampered than you might guess by my sour expression and your own cliche expectations of what one parent working in the toughest business in the world could provide, I was picked up and cuddled by the most beautiful and successful people in the world. That was all very nice.

HARMON. So what was the problem?

YVONNE. I saw kisses. I was a little girl on the set and I asked my mother, I said, those people kissing do they love each other? My mother said no, it's all fake, that the kisses are make-believe and that often the people kissing not only hardly knew one another but more often than not found the other person revolting.

HARMON. There are real kisses. I can prove it.

YVONNE. I never kiss. (He kisses her.)

HARMON. I love you.

YVONNE. It's not realistic you should love me.

HARMON. Believe it, what do you have to lose?

YVONNE. How do I know you're not the villain? Yes, that you'll whisk me away and the minute I relax, ditch me? How do I know you're not really from *Mean To Me*? I mean you know the lines well enough, don't you? Maybe this is all one big set-up. Maybe what you really have instead of a hope house is a slave ship. Or worse than a thrill-kill Romeo, maybe you're a Jack the Ripper of the recluse circuit. You'd have found your perfect victim, wouldn't you — brittle, combative party girl hiding out between trends, waiting to see what will be the next big fad before I decide on any new hair color. This one hasn't grown out very well I'm afraid, and I think about it all the time. That's the kind of girl I am. No, I'm not ashamed to admit my little flaws, my solipsism, my lassitude, my empty easy dreary despair. If these are the traits you're looking for in your bride then you need look no further.

HARMON. Go get your things.

YVONNE. I can't leave my mother. My mother and I pretend everything's all right and it is all right.

HARMON. She wants you to go. You're her obstruction. I'm taking the obstruction away. You have to be a good sport and come away with me.

YVONNE. I used to sponge the kisses and the words off her lips with a wet washcloth.

HARMON. Go and get whatever things you'll need for a few weeks.

YVONNE. I don't want to go to that place. What does everyone do, sit around singing from the Joan Baez songbook?

HARMON. Just go and come back. *(Exit Yvonne. Enter Selma.)*

SELMA. Hi.

HARMON. Are you doing all right here?

SELMA. Oh, yeah, and I'm thinking of reading the Bible out to Jean. Neither of us have ever read it and everyone says it's very good. *(Removing a box of baking soda from her purse.)* The sixteen-ounce box of Arm and Hammer baking soda is thirty cents cheaper here. That's a big difference. I'm not stealing so much anymore, or just a little, a can or two every once in a while. Or coupons off the sides of containers to get the dollar refund. It's a horrible feeling wondering if you're paying too much for everything. You hold something in your hand and look at it, look at its price, and you think is it really worth it? I suppose if you're with someone they can tell you. I had a boyfriend once but we hardly touched and now, if he's alive, I wonder if he even

29

thinks about me. Probably not. *(Enter Yvonne with a bag.)*
YVONNE. I can't go away with you. I don't know enough about you.
HARMON. Like what?
YVONNE. Is your body nice?
HARMON. When I was at divinity school I couldn't get financial aid so I got a job at the art school, posing. It paid well and seemed as good an excuse as any to stand around nude.
YVONNE. Then it must be good.
HARMON. I could take my clothes off for you so you can see.
YVONNE. Well, maybe later.
SELMA. Here are some cookies I wrapped for you.
YVONNE. Bye, Betty.
SELMA. Goodbye. *(Harmon and Yvonne exit. Jean enters.)*
JEAN. Did Yvonne leave?
SELMA. Just now.
JEAN. I'm glad. Some things actually do work out the way you plan them. *(She sings a few stanzas of a song like "Bye, Bye Blackbird."*)*

Scene 2

Afternoon. Flowers in vases.

SELMA. *(Closing the Bible.)* The End.
JEAN. How beautiful. I love an uplifting story. If I could hear one a day I might forgive the world its transgressions.
SELMA. Tea?
JEAN. No, thanks. Well that was fun, now before they get here we've got our work cut out for us. What are we up to, honey?
SELMA. I have up to —
JEAN. Just do it, do it and I'll catch up and pipe in. I just need a second to tune in. Go ahead, just start.
SELMA. Because this was a long long time ago and I was a young and beautiful movie actress, I had many millionaires offering me their hands in marriage.

---

* See Special Note on Songs and Recordings on copyright page.

JEAN. Oh, I see what we're up to, how the bills got paid.

SELMA. They loved me and proposed to me every Christmas Eve whether they were married or not. They didn't mind that I had a little girl, they even grew fond of Yvonne and bought her dresses and toys and instead of one father she had ten!

JEAN. The voice is all wrong. I've got to say that, Sel, it's just wrong.

SELMA. *(Overlapping Jean.)* Higher or lower?

JEAN. What?

SELMA. My voice. Higher or lower?

JEAN. Just go on and I'll concentrate. You're doing great. I'll store up my tips, go on.

SELMA. When we lived in New York, Yvonne and I would periodically go to one of the living millionaires for lunch. Usually the San Remo or the El Dorado ... And you could see the whole city, how beautiful it is from a great height!

JEAN. Jesus. And, Betty, you've *got* to get rid of that bit about the view. I couldn't see it! Let's keep some iota of believability — please.

SELMA. I thought you were going to let me talk.

JEAN. Who's stopping you? Go on, let's hear that one you've perfected: how I fell in love. Go on, hit it.

SELMA. Not if you're going to mock it.

JEAN. Betty, darling, sweet good Betty who makes all the sweets a person could sensibly eat, kiddie-party cupcakes with three-quarters icing, I could not mock you on a bet, not for gold. I have every faith your version of things is going to be heartily embraced — people are going to do the hula around it with joy — believe me. Just stick in somewhere my favorite Balzac quote would you? "Corruption is the greatest power in the world, you will be made to feel it everywhere." Stick that in, Betty, would you, for me.

SELMA. I'm doing the best I can.

JEAN. I know you are, I'm sorry. Selma, are you there? Sel. Sneeze or something so I know you're alive.

SELMA. Everything is very hard for me. You don't know what that's like, Jean, to have it be hard to even say what you think, to not even know what you think, to have to take what other people think, to not know what's right.

JEAN. You're right, I'm horrible. But please don't cry. Now you go on but you just raise your voice a little, that's all you have to do, not higher or lower, just louder, okay?

SELMA. I can't go on now, I'm upset.

JEAN. Now, I said I'm sorry, Betty.

31

SELMA. No, not that. You got a letter today. I didn't read it to you. *(Enter Yvonne.)*

YVONNE. Sweetie pie, I'm home! I've missed you!

JEAN. I've missed you too. Give me another kiss.

YVONNE. Another one for me. You look so pretty.

JEAN. I do? I'm the same. I haven't changed a thing, have we, Betty?

SELMA. Oh, we've been busy.

YVONNE. You look so pretty too, Betty.

SELMA. Oh, I don't.

JEAN. Where's Larry? Isn't Larry coming?

YVONNE. Oh, he'll be here in a second. He stopped to buy some flowers but I see you don't need any.

SELMA. I've been working in the garden. Keeps my fingers busy.

YVONNE. These are awfully pretty, Selma. Anyway, act surprised when he walks in with them because I was supposed to say he was going for gas.

JEAN. Good, Betty, that'll give you a chance to practice your acting. We've been very busy around here, we've turned into a veritable conservatory or taxidermist's parlor I don't know which.

SELMA. I like your dress, Yvonne.

YVONNE. I feel like a badly updated version of Botticelli's *Primavera*. But he likes it, what can I do? If Bobby could see me in this get-up he'd gag.

SELMA. You look great.

YVONNE. I guess I really do look good. I thought going to that place and listening to everyone's problems would give me an ear infection but it's had the opposite effect. I feel great! I don't know if it's just a big ego trip or what, offering my two cents but I realize I'm a lot smarter and more sensitive than I'd been giving myself credit for. And I cook. I just throw things in a pot and everyone loves it. At first I thought Larry was going to be Mr. Bossy Chieftan but he's really not. He gives jobs to everyone and stays in the background if he sees something working well on its own. Maybe because I'm a new face there I've become popular and people come asking for me. A lot of people's lives that look to them like complete catastrophes really aren't and they just need to be told so or shaken a little bit — I'm sort of good at that — and it's not a depressing place at all. It is really quite lovely. Selma, I don't know how you brought yourself to leave and, speaking of that, you are very well-missed and highly spoken of. I told everyone your new name and they were very intrigued.

JEAN. And you're happy with Larry?

YVONNE. Oh God yes: When he came here I thought he was a psychopath but then I used to think everyone was a psychopath, anyone who seemed even remotely happy or content I thought must be completely out of their minds! You know, it occurred to me in the car coming over here: well, maybe my appreciation of people is shallow and I'm happy now with the bright side just as I was perhaps shallowly disgusted with the dark but, guess what, who cares. Maybe all we do over there is pop-psychologizing and pseudo-religious cheerleading and maybe authorities are going to pop in tomorrow and close us down but until then I'm happy! And you know, I never wanted children. I thought bringing another living thing into this barbaric world was an act of unforgivable sadism but now I want twenty. I told Larry and he choked but he'll just have to get used to the idea: I want twenty and that's that.

JEAN. I only have a second so I'll ask you outright — do you blame me, Yvonne, did I make you sick of the world before you got a taste of it?

YVONNE. I love you.

JEAN. I know, I know but that's not the question. I know there were just the two of us and maybe I made you eat my opinions before you could shop for your own. I'm feeling terribly guilty, Yvonne.

YVONNE. Well, you did lie to me. You told me everything was shitty and it's not, not all of it, not everyone; everything's not a sham.

JEAN. I never said it was! Betty knows I'm just a bluff, don't you, Betty?

YVONNE. Sometimes I didn't even know if it was you or me talking, only you had a more interesting past to draw on.

JEAN. When we lived in New York you were so popular I don't think you stayed home one night. But now you're lucky in love and I'm so pleased for you!

YVONNE. But you don't believe it.

JEAN. I do! Don't forget I played women in love almost exclusively.

YVONNE. In movies.

JEAN. I tried to have a relationship that could last but there were no good examples to follow — and in the end it was only the old impotent monkey-millionaires who could fantasize about my siren appeal that still looked after me with any affection. Of course I wanted to be in love — *it just didn't work out!*

YVONNE. So you do think everything is shitty.

JEAN. Well, isn't it? You wait and see, you're happy today but happy has a way of skipping town like no other rogue and then you'll really see how familiar the hopeless can look when their chief representative meets you in the mirror every time you look there! Yvonne, I didn't mean that. I'm happy you're in love, it was my biggest wish — a selfish wish — so I could live with myself. I love you and of course Larry loves you and will stay in love with you and you with him — I'm acting badly but that's because I'm sincere. I got out of Hollywood because of you, Yvonne — it's true. Whether the business was corrupt or the camera got tired of me was really not the issue — no one loved me and I just couldn't stand to see myself alone in that town or have you see me that way. Did you know I could hear you from my room — or did you think I was deaf too? It frightened me to see all my worst feelings alive in you but you weren't playing me, Yvonne, that's not me! I was innocent once and it was taken somehow and shared with crowds of people and now I want it back! I just don't see things in the popular way but Betty insists I'll be happier if I change my opinion. Is that the brave new world we heard about, everyone taking happy pills? It frightens me, quite frankly, blind happiness. What do you make of it, you're happy now, do you feel safe or will it be taken from you suddenly and your breath with it?

YVONNE. I don't know. *(Enter Harmon with flowers.)*

HARMON. It's me again.

JEAN. Flowers for me!

HARMON. How did you know, you can't see them.

JEAN. But I can smell them.

HARMON. From over there?

JEAN. Just hand me the flowers.

HARMON. I see a lot of competition.

YVONNE. They're Selma's, from the garden. Aren't they pretty?

JEAN. Yvonne, here's your chance for me to use that vase you gave me you say I never use. Go in the kitchen and fill it and take a long time.

SELMA. I'll go stir the cookies. *(Yvonne and Selma exit.)*

JEAN. Listen, I need to know whether you really love my little girl. I don't want Yvonne to wake up one afternoon and find she's been dropped from the mission with a brood of twenty!

HARMON. Oh she told you that, did she? Well, the answer is no, I don't want twenty children, it's too fantastic a sum. But as far as loving Yvonne goes, I do, completely. But I'm not as shocked or

34

surprised about it as you or Yvonne seem to be. I planned to find my true love and I did. I was raised without a religion so I made up my own and it's easy to practice. There are no candles, no special robes or holidays or long impossible-to-remember prayers in languages people don't speak anymore. The only rule is to love everyone. Here, I'm still holding these flowers. These are for you.

JEAN. Betty's been able to make things grow from the weeds back there. It's just a hobby, but it's sort of miraculous.

HARMON. They're very nice.

JEAN. I don't think she steals anymore but then she's always running out to the store for something. I guess it's just sugar. She really is very sweet, if I can't sleep she comes to my room and reads to me. She told me the whole story of her childhood. And then we're working together on this thing. Oh, we have a high time. *(Enter Yvonne and Selma.)*

YVONNE. Selma's said there's been a letter from Bobby.

JEAN. *(Hands it to Harmon.)* Here; you read it.

HARMON. "Dear Yvonne and Jean, I have terrible news. I'm writing from Paris where after Gregory complaining of one ailment upon another and my mostly ignoring them because — like me, I figured, he's just a big hypochondriac, but then it turns out to be all real, and after demanding to be taken to Paris for what he kept referring to as the Rock Hudson treatment, he's dead. It as of yet has no reality though his parents have been quick to accept it, informing me immediately they will contest nothing in Gregory's will no matter what property or inheritance he has left me which is rather civil of them given I refused to accompany the body, I was just too freaked out. The terror I feel is not disease-related because our sex life had an inadvertently safety-conscious repertoire. Nevertheless, a gruesome abyss has opened for me of widowhood and the black mark of death. I'm still holding the little piece of paper of our itinerary which finishes up appropriately, it turns out, in Land's End. Why is it the extra sweater I packed and lugged needlessly has more weight, more reality, takes up more room in my consciousness than the death of someone who loved me? As small recompense I tell myself that my moral torpor makes me a man of my times. If I had the knack I'd turn it all into a folk song and sing it in sawdust-strewn taverns. Instead I'm packed for Connecticut where you can reach me at these numbers and this address. Love, Bobby."

YVONNE. We'll call him immediately. He'll come and work at

the shelter. I need him there, he needs it too. Poor Bobby, it's worse to lose someone you don't really love, they can leave you their whole inheritance and you're still left with nothing. *(She exits.)*

JEAN. I want to talk to Bobby too. Call him and tell him we'll pick him up. *(Jean exits.)*

SELMA. I don't want to play Jean. I disagree with what she says about the world.

HARMON. I'm thinking of handing the shelter over to Yvonne. She has the energy of ten of me right now. And I'm so distracted by my love for her. I just want to stare at her all day.

SELMA. Does it weaken you when your dreams come true?

HARMON. No.

SELMA. In my dreams I always thought the day would come when I'd be someone for somebody. I see now you can't anticipate who that will be. We're told a terrible loneliness is waiting for our bodies in our graves and that we should rush to have pleasure while we're still alive but I think when you live that way you see that until you love someone you can't find pleasure in anything. I'm not leaving here. I'm staying with Jean. We love each other. I know she talks to me like a maidservant but that doesn't bother me. I'm glad to be at the center of someone's attention and have someone at the center of mine. Everyone wants to be the center of attention at least once even for a minute if just to get a taste of the sweetness we get in heaven. *(Enter Yvonne and Jean.)*

YVONNE. Bobby's a mess, Larry. I think we should go get him immediately, Mother understands and we'll be back, we'll call and make a new date. Sorry, Selma, did I say you look very pretty? Larry, let me drive, I'm too upset to sit still, don't worry, I'll be careful. Now, you're not mad, are you, this abrupt come and go?

JEAN. Absolutely not, you know I love Bobby, give him a hundred kisses from me and tell him I want to see him.

HARMON. Now don't forget we're counting on you to make an appearance at the shelter. It would give so many people there so much pleasure, you don't seem to know it but you're very much loved.

JEAN. Oh well, just tell them there's just a little shadow left. Jeannie the shadow, right, Betty? I'm sending Betty as me, it'll be very avant-garde. Let me kiss you both goodbye. Here's an extra kiss goodbye.

SELMA. Bye. *(Harmon and Yvonne exit.)*

JEAN. That's the shortest visit I've ever had. But I'm glad. I'm glad because now I can die. You can't die if you think someone's depending on you for something.

SELMA. You're not going to die so just be quiet.

JEAN. I'll kill myself when I'm alone.

SELMA. You won't.

JEAN. No? Well, maybe I won't. Maybe I'll just die of something indeterminate like they do in the movies. Is there no wine left in this bottle? I guess I'm not so thirsty.

SELMA. Jean, I've been thinking and I've decided you're right, that it's stupid to whitewash the way things are, that the worst version is the truest version.

JEAN. What? I never said that.

SELMA. Yes, you've been right all along. Give me another chance to play you.

JEAN. You were doing fine, Selma, I didn't tell you to change.

SELMA. I'm dimming all the lights so I only see light and dark.

JEAN. What? Why?

SELMA. So I see like you, what you see, so I'm more in character.

JEAN. What was that?

SELMA. I lit a match. I'm lighting a candle. I want to be like an oracle, telling only the truth. Now you listen to me and I'll do you. When I came to Hollywood it was *its time* like Florence in the time of the de Medicis or Egypt in the time of the pyramids, it was — what is it you call it? — a confluence of time, and that only happens here and there in eternity, sporadic and inspired. I was a face not yet twenty and in the flickering light I gave my life.

JEAN. That's not bad!

SELMA. The studio head said, "She's pretty," as if he'd been told I was a cripple and now on inspection thought it was a miracle I could walk at all. Having passed that test I was put in mugging school where you're taught to mug out expressions for every emotion, making faces and copying them. And I was good at it. I was such a blank with no life experience to get in the way — that it was easy for me. With my first pot of money I bought huge thick white towels and wrapped myself in them, newborn to luxury. They're grey and threadbare now, used to soak up water when the ceiling leaks. Do it as cheaply and quickly as possible is the code in Never-Never Land as in the world. And it never made any difference whether it was good or bad because everything was *presold*. Just so long as you kept up all that fake optimism which sells like beer and is stupid as Canada is large. Those who believe in nothing, my dear, have the greatest need for faith so the producers were always the most rabid advocates of the happy ending. It was *de rigueur*, I was always a part of the unseen unhappy ending. "Play Yourself," they screamed at me. It got to the point where I was practically the last person on earth I wanted to play. But that's solved because after your life's become a sideshow even you've seen once too often, you're handed your furry hat and told you can just drop dead. *(Pause.)*

JEAN. I'm astonished. I didn't realize you had so much … power. The things you said. Where did you get all that stuff?

SELMA. From you, you said it, I just remember it.

JEAN. It's so horrible Selma, to hear that from someone else! You should just forget all that and go back to your other story, the one you made up, how I fell in love with my husband, do that one.

SELMA. You can't decide everything's good suddenly.

JEAN. Why not?

SELMA. Because it has to come from inside, not from outside in.

JEAN. Oh hogwash, I'll say what I like. Go back, I tell you, to your old track.

SELMA. No.

JEAN. Why?

SELMA. I don't want to misrepresent you.

JEAN. I can't stand to listen to any more of that bile! My time is finished; I just want to go when I go without this sour taste in my mouth. That's all I want, please give me that, can't you, Selma? You can stay here as long as you like, it's your home.

SELMA. I know.

JEAN. So how do we solve this problem, Sel, I say you play me my way and you want to play me as me. Why don't you just pick some moment with some sweetness to it and do that?

SELMA. It has to be more than one isolated moment. God can't be so miserable and wish us so little as one solitary moment to live on.

JEAN. How about a love scene. Do that, you like that.

SELMA. But I'll tell the truth.

JEAN. Yes, tell the truth.

SELMA. But what part of the truth — that the man you loved had a negligible career, was being eased out of Hollywood with the subtlety of a steam shovel?

JEAN. It wasn't his fault they were through with him! And when they are through with you they are through with you. And I forgive him and I forgive everyone. I'm sick of being angry, sick to death of it! Oh Selma, should I not have called you Betty? I can call you Jean if you like that, I don't care anymore, we can both be Jean or you can call me Betty.

SELMA. No, it's fine the way it is. I'll be Betty or Selma. And you just be Jean. I don't want to play you. Play yourself.

JEAN. Yes then I will. I'll play me.

SELMA. The devil has only one flaw: he's stupid. Because if he was smart he would choose to be good.

JEAN. Okay okay, enough already with the devils and angels. I'm going to do my love scene. I just need to focus on something good and stick to it, the time before the kisses became indistinguishable. The first time I was kissed, for real, off-camera, it was very still as if we were indoors but we were outside and there was no wind, no wind machine, no sound of people shhsing, only my own mind narrating the whole thing solemnly, breathlessly, *so this is the kiss, so this is the embrace,* alone with someone without wondering whether you'll be shown to bad advantage, and you hear the heart beat and it's like a shocking bit of dialogue, that beat, and it's beating for you, and if the other person says I love you — as he did — you see yourself for the first time and you're reinvented, more beautiful than any magician cameraman's kindness, and if you love the other person — even for an instant, or a month, as I did — and you say so — you say I love you — and you think, yes, now it's happening, now it's happening for me, youth, beauty, spring, everything wasn't cut off from me — I was a fool to think it was — my heart is saved at the last minute by this bit of light — flickering so bright I open my eyes and see an end to the night.

End of Play

PROPERTY LIST

Jam, yogurt, spoon (YVONNE)
Letter with postcard and newspaper clipping (YVONNE)
Paper, pen (YVONNE)
Tea service (YVONNE)
Handbag (YVONNE)
Cookies (YVONNE)
Wine, glasses (SELMA)
Letter (YVONNE)
Cough drops (SELMA)
Sandwiches (YVONNE)
Purse with baking soda (SELMA)
Suitcase (YVONNE)
Bible (SELMA)
Flowers (HARMON)